SIMON

by Arthur Fanning

Published by Light Technology Publishing
P.O. Box 1526
Sedona, AZ 86336

Published by Light Technology Publishing
P.O. Box 1526
Sedona, AZ 86336
(602) 282-6523 Fax (602) 282-4130
ISBN 0-929-385-32-2

Cover illustration by
Penny Bushman
Cover Design and Chapter Illustrations by
Joanna Heikens

Mission Possible Commercial Printing

Dedicated to Mom

"I love you..."

Arthur

ONE

The old man sat at the edge of the sea, his feet in the water and his sandals beside him. An old, gray, weather-beaten cowboy hat sheltered his head from the morning sun while the waves washed the edges of his faded red and yellow Bermuda shorts. A dolphin swam into the cove directly toward him, beached itself, and nuzzled gently against his left leg.

Reaching down with his leathery left hand, the old man gently stroked the dolphin's silky smooth skin. "I'm glad you came," the old man said, staring into the eyes of the dolphin. "I've missed you."

"I am always aware of your needs, and you should know by now that you are always in our thoughts," the dolphin communicated to the old man.

"Yes, I know. But I feel better when I can touch you and talk to you at the same time." The old man sighed a very long and slow sigh.

"Introspection, no matter how painful, is the key to growth. You are aware of that, of course," the dolphin transmitted.

"Yes."

A blissful peace settled over the secluded cove. Waves stopped breaking the way they had before the dolphin had come and were rolling ever so gently toward the shore, as if ashamed of themselves for having to disturb the meeting of these old friends. As though ancient guardians of some mystic rite, two giant blue whales swam fifty yards offshore.

The young boy, with shaggy brown hair mostly covering his forehead and glasses so dusty he could barely see, watched cautiously from his hiding place in the sedge grass of the sand dune, his eyes wild in disbelief. What had started out as one silver dolphin had become more than fifty with two whales just a little way off. What made things even more unbelievable was that it looked as though the silver dolphin was talking to all of them, including the old man, as though he was giving a speech.

It was noon now, and the dolphins had been with the old man since dawn. The silver dolphin looked into the old man's eyes and projected the message, *"We'll be leaving now. May your thoughts move in peace."* Then it made a curious clicking sound, and as if on signal, dolphins and whales leaped high into the air. The whales smashed the surface of the water with their huge bodies, sending a crashing ka-whoosh! through the air. Simultaneously, all the dolphins sent a machine-gun staccato of clicks into the air, spun on their tails, and dove away. The last to leave was the silver-gray one, the one that had been first to arrive. He winked at the old man and said, *"I'll get back to you (click, click)."*

With a wave of his hand, the old man responded, "See you later, Simon."

The sun blinked, and the old man instantly materialized beside the boy in the sedge grass. "There are only a few people in the world to whom the dolphins talk. Did you know that?" His voice shattered the silence of the boy's thoughts.

"How did you do that?" the boy asked, visibly shaken both by the loudness of the old man's voice and by his sudden appearance beside him.

"We knew you were here, Freemore," the old man said, completely ignoring the question. "The dolphins wouldn't have stayed if they hadn't wanted you to know. Come and walk the beach with me." He extended his tanned leather hand to the boy.

Because of his eyes, his blue-gold eyes that flecked red-gold like the sun when he talked, the boy instinctively knew he could trust this old man with the worn-out cowboy hat and leathery face. Taking his hand, they walked off the sand dune and along the edge of the water.

"How do you know my name?" the boy asked.

"Lets just say I knew your parents before you were born."

"What's your name, sir?"

"Just think of me as an old friend."

Squinting from the reflection of the sun coming off the water, the boy looked up at the old man and commented, "Boy, that sure is an old hat."

"Serves it's purpose. Serves it's purpose." The man lifted his hat with his left hand, patted his bald head with his right, and continued. "Keep the hat on and it keeps the top smooth. See?"

"Not like your face, huh?" the boy said matter-of-factly.

The old man's laugh scattered the sandpipers dancing along the shore. The leather face folded neatly into its creases, and the eyes flecked gold. "Right you are, lad. Right you are," he said.

The boy brightened at the laugh and asked, "How come the dolphins came out of the water to you like that? Did you train them?"

"Train them? No, no, no! That silver-gray one that you saw–well, he is the one that is doing the training, not me."

"Training? I don't understand. Do you mean the dolphin was actually talking to you? I thought I was just imagining it."

"He was talking to all of us."

"What was he talking about?"

"Oh, about things that you know now and that a lot of grown-ups have forgotten, things that the dolphins haven't forgotten. The dolphins know. And that silver-gray one knows more than the others."

"What kinds of things?"

"Things such as flying dreams, things such as our reason for being here on earth in the first place, things such as how we manage to make it work even though we pretend we don't know."

"I don't get it," Freemore said, watching his feet as they walked.

"You will someday, son. You will. The important thing is to remember not to forget. Most adults have forgotten and want their children to forget, too. They were told to forget, and it seemed to work out well for them. They don't begin to question until they realize there must be a purpose to life. For many, this realization doesn't come in one lifetime."

Looking up, Freemore asked, "Can you teach

me to talk to the dolphins, please?"

"I don't know," the old man replied. "That'll be up to Simon."

"Simon? Is . . . is that the dolphin? The silver-gray one?"

The old man nodded his head. "Beautiful, isn't he?" he asked, gazing out across the water.

"Boy, I'll say! Please, let me go with you," Freemore begged. "I'll be here every day. I won't forget. I won't let anybody make me forget. Can I go? Please?"

"Meet me here tomorrow and we'll see what Simon has to say. Okay?"

"Okay!" A broad grin spread across the young boy's face.

TWO

It seemed as though only yesterday that he had met the old man on the beach, not thirty-five years ago. He could not remember why he had not gone back the next day, but he was sure there had been a reason.

Now it was dusk. As they traveled south in their Winnebego along Highway 101, the setting sun was casting its last golden-red spears across the water. The light cotton puff clouds being carried toward the shore by the wind reflected the red-gold rays.

"Maybe you weren't really ready, Freemore," his wife interrupted his reverie.

"Phagan, you are really incredible! How did you know I was thinking about that old man?"

"I can hear your thoughts, honey. Remember?"

"I'm glad I don't have anything to hide," Freemore chuckled.

For a period of time, they rode in silence, each lost in his own thoughts. As twilight descended upon them, finally Freemore spoke. "I heard someplace that there are no such things as secrets," he said, squirming and trying to stretch out his legs.

"Not with you around, that's for sure." Phagan looked up from her driving and smiled at her husband. "Let's stop and get something to eat," she suggested. "We should be pretty close by now. Maybe another mile or so."

She drove into a turnout along the highway and prepared submarine sandwiches, then poured for each a glass of red wine.

Sitting at the small dinette table, they looked out the side window. The view was magnificent. A waxing moon under a bright, starlit sky cast her beams on the gentle swells of the ocean. From their vantage point high on the cliff, they could almost feel the ocean communicating with the moon. At length, Freemore said, "You know, Phagan, it's really crazy."

"What's crazy?"

"How, especially on a night such as this, can man contemplate war and the destruction it brings? Can't they see that even the moon and the ocean cooperate and don't compete. I have to find that dolphin, Phagan," he added resolutely. "I just have to. The old man told me that the dolphins know."

"I've done some strange things, Freemore, but this takes the cake, bar none. I mean, who would ever think to go looking for a dolphin to find the answers to the meaning of life? Why couldn't you have gone after some guru on a mountaintop in Tibet or something? That, at least, is acceptable in some circles. But a dolphin? A silver dolphin? Do you know how many dolphins are out there?" she asked, gesturing toward the moonlit ocean. "There has to be a million of them, and you're looking for one. One!"

"Now, what brought all this about?" Freemore asked, glancing sharply at the woman sitting across from him.

"I love you," she said, "and you know it. I just don't want you to waste yourself on some godforsaken quest for the Holy Grail. I know this is going to upset you . . ."

"Don't say it then."

"Bull! You know as well as I that I'm going to say it. I have to, if we are to be honest with one another."

"Do I have to listen?"

"Only if you expect me to be friendly tonight."

Sighing, Freemore sat back in the seat and stared our across the water. "Go ahead then," he said, chuckling, "but let us not be too honest."

"Are you absolutely sure you didn't fall asleep on the beach and simply dream of seeing an old man talking to dolphins?" Phagan asked, a concerned look furrowing her brow. "I mean, it was so long ago. Can you be positive your not confusing reality with a childhood fantasy?"

"I'm positive."

"That's it? Just 'I'm positive?' No explanation, no nothing, just, 'I'm positive?'"

Freemore bit into his sandwich and chewed it slowly. After washing it down with a sip from his glass, he said, "I told you before, I have this feeling that I let the old man down. I mean, I begged him to let me go with him the next day, and he agreed to take me, but I didn't show up. For the life of me, I can't remember why I didn't go, but I didn't."

"You probably knew it was a dream. That was why you didn't go."

"It wasn't a dream, I'm telling you!"

"Okay, okay." She went around to his side of the table and pulled his head onto her shoulder. Stroking his hair with her hand, what little he had left, she said, "I'm glad you at least listened."

THREE

When Freemore awoke, the sun was streaming through the rear window of the "Winnie." Phagan, still asleep next to him, looked like a goddess in the flesh. "Who would have believed that a woman such as this could fall in love with me," he whispered to himself. He slipped quietly out of bed and pulled on his clothes.

Going to the kitchen area, he put on some coffee and had started cooking some bacon and eggs when Phagan opened her eyes and stretched. "Mmmmmmmmm," she murmured sleepily. "That smells great mixed with the smell of the salt air coming through the window, doesn't it?" Stepping into her slippers, she donned a bright yellow robe and headed for the kitchen. Like angel hands, her golden hair caressed her cheeks.

Freemore smiled proudly at her, then looked out the window and said, "No contest, sun!"

"Thank you for the compliment . . . and so early, too," she told him, moving over next to him.

"You most assuredly deserve it." Freemore gazed approvingly at his wife, then asked, "Are you hungry?"

"Famished."

"Great. Let's eat, and then we'll look around. I have a feeling we're pretty close to that cove. You can do the dishes when we get back."

"You cooked, so I'll wash. No problem."

They ate quietly, each wrapped in his own thoughts. But Freemore knew his thoughts were easily accessible to her.

Putting down her fork, Phagan said, "I can see you're ready. Just let me get dressed and I'll be right with you."

"Okay," Freemore replied. "I'll wait outside."

The sky was a radiant blue with tiny pearls of clouds trying to unite. Freemore walked to the edge of the cliff for a closer view of the ocean, the mother of all life, and it was there Phagan found him staring intently below. "What do you see?" she asked inquisitively, putting her arm around his waist.

"Look." Freemore pointed to a spot in the distance.

"That's the cove we've been looking for. That's it!" He sounded excited.

"Are you sure?"

"Positive!" he declared.

"There's that 'positive' again," she said teasingly.

"I'm telling you, that's the cove," he insisted. "Look there. The sand dune is just where I said it was, back away from the shore. This is it." Turning to look at her, he added, "There are no accidents, Phagan. No accidents."

"Well, how do we get down there?" she asked. "This cliff is pretty steep to climb down."

"There should be a small footpath about three-fourths of a mile back that leads through some sycamores to a winding path set in the cliff."

"Let's go then," Phagan said.

They walked quietly along the road, the ocean hidden from their view by the span of tall sycamores, the trees at least fifty feet high. A squirrel scampered among their branches, announcing their presence to the invisible forest creatures, as they turned into the grove of trees. A swarm of silvery bees with rainbow wings flew high overhead in search of nectar.

The path they followed curved gently downward, hugging the white cliff wall. As they exited the sycamore grove, a sense of peace and tranquility descended upon them. Directly before them, fifty yards out to sea, a brilliant lilac colored light shone. They had reached the sand dune with the sedge grass.

"This place is beautiful, Freemore, absolutely beautiful," Phagan remarked in awe. "How did you ever find it?"

"I can't remember," he replied, looking out over the water. "When I was a child I stumbled upon it. Didn't you get the feeling there were guardians at some invisible gate as we came through that grove of sycamores? I'll bet thousands of people have picnicked in there and none have found the path that leads down the side of the cliff."

"I feel as if I am dreaming." Phagan walked up to her husband and took his hand. With her other hand, she pointed off into the distance. "Look at that light," she said. "What an incredible glow! What is it?"

"I don't know," Freemore replied, "but I have a feeling we are going to find out."

Getting larger, the shimmering lilac glow rose from the depths of the ocean floor, its color vibrating between shimmering silver and shimmering violet.

"Thoughts are things." The sound cracked through the air and exploded in the stand of sycamores on the cliff. *"When the student is ready, the teacher appears."* The voice, or sound, or whatever it was, now had a soft musical quality, lilting, yet authoritative.

"Phagan, did you hear that?" Freemore almost whispered.

"Hear it? I felt it. Every atom of my body feels as though it is vibrating to that tone. It is a beautiful feeling. Can you feel it?"

Looking at her, Freemore could tell she was indeed experiencing something extremely pleasant. Her face had taken on a pink glow, and a hint of silvery sparkle was streaking out of her eyes. "You look radiant, honey, simply radiant," he told her.

"I feel radiant," she said. "I'm picking up something inside me now, like a translation of the tones. Can you feel it? It's incredible."

"I can't feel anythi . . .

"Will you look at that!" he suddenly exclaimed.

A silver-gray dolphin crashed through the surface of the sea and leaped a thousand feet into the air, the spray sparkling gold in the morning sun. Another followed, then another and another. Freemore counted thirteen, in all, twisting, turning, spinning in the air. They stared knowingly at the two creatures standing on the shore before diving back into the sea, then playing on the surface.

"You create your own world," came the voice from the water. *"All of it. Every bit of it. Your inner self rejoices in its creation, for it is doing what you have asked it to do. Ask and you shall receive. May your thoughts move in peace (click, click)."*

"Simon? Are you the dolphin called Simon?" Freemore screamed at the top of his lungs.

"If you need a name, that is one I have been known to use, among others."

"How . . ."

"You are experiencing another aspect of consciousness, Freemore. And since this is new to you, we must end this conversation here. You will soon realize your time is not our time. Take Phagan back to the motor home now. She needs her rest, and so do you. You will have a busy day tomorrow. I'll get back to you. May your thoughts move in peace (click, click)."

With that, the dolphins dove out of sight, and the lilac glow faded from the sea. In the distance, two giant whales rose high into the air, shattering the surface of the sea as they dove back into the water.

"Phagan, are you okay?" Freemore asked.

"I don't know," she answered, her voice shaking slightly. "I feel kind of weaky."

"Weaky? What's weaky?"

"My whole body is sort of shaking inside, as though thousands–no, millions–of tiny earthquakes are rocking inside me."

Concerned, Freemore said, "We'd better get

you back to the Winnie. Do you want me to carry you?"

"I'll be okay," she told him. Just hold me for a minute before we leave. Okay?"

Tenderly he drew her to him and held her in his arms. He could feel her body trembling. "Are you all right?" he asked again, for now she was crying on his shoulder.

"Yes," she managed between sobs. "I love you, Freemore."

"I love you, too, Phagan."

The walk back to the Winnie was quiet and peaceful. The air was still. The colors of the trees and sky blended one with the other, cooperating, not competing. The essence of the universe sang all around the two walking quietly hand in hand, and they knew love was the force holding the universe together. It was dusk.

FOUR

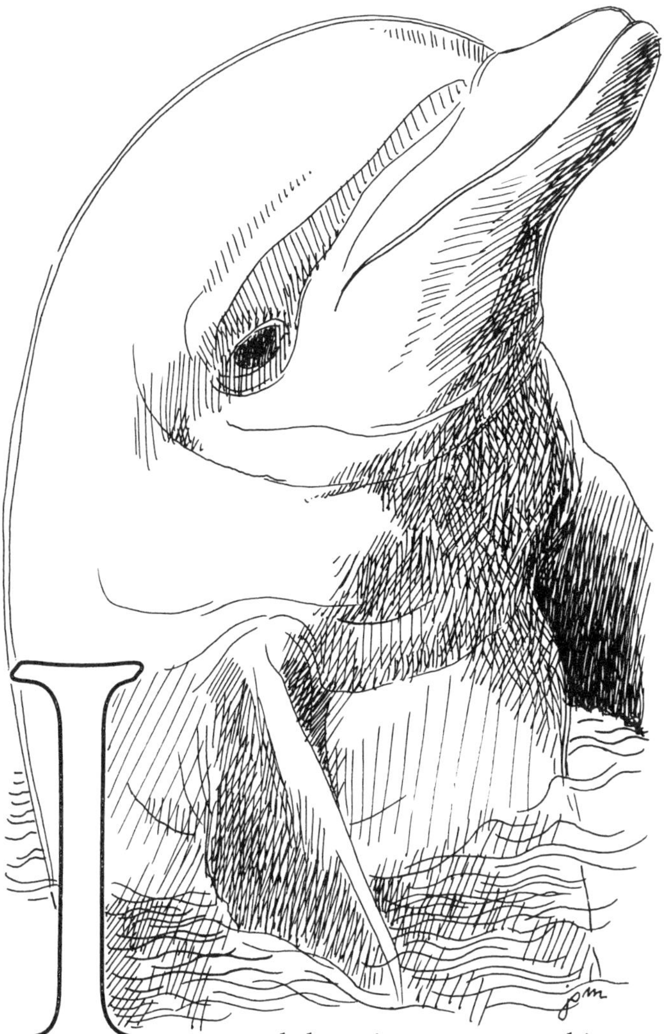

It seemed that Simon was speaking. *"Your best work is done in your dreams. Your body is the physical manifestation of your*

thoughts. The emotional experience is that portion of the universal flux that is reborn in the frame of reference to which you refer as reincarnation. The emotional body is that portion reincarnated in time as the physical body, or more accurately, a thought form, your own thought form, for on all planes your thoughts, emotions, and beliefs create the reality that you see and experience."

"Talk about divine justice," Freemore said to himself. "Who am I kidding? Nobody is going to believe this. Am I crazy?"

The voice in his head continued. *"The fact is, man has to learn responsibility, and as you are finding out, the responsibility is to that inner self that knew how to grow you from a fetus to an adult. Or are you taking all the credit for that?"*

"What credit?" Freemore asked.

"Do you think for one moment that you could consciously control all the bodily processes necessary for your physical growth? You would have one hell of a time trying to get any sleep, I'll tell you that. It is the inner self that controls those functions, and it is the same inner self that creates exactly what you experience. That is its function. The record is kept in the pineal gland, among others. It is a requirement of the inner self that it fulfills all your requests. And it does, for the inner self has direct contact with the forces you refer to as God."

Incredulous, Freemore asked, "If the inner self does all this stuff, then why is the world so messed up?"

"Be careful what you see, Freemore," came the reply, *"for you create your own reality. If all you see is a mess, then know that you have created that for yourself. The world is a mirror of your beliefs. It is a mirror of what you yourself are creating. Believe it."*

"This could really get complicated. I mean, you do know that, don't you? Who in the world is going to be able follow all of it?"

"You don't have to be able to follow it. Simply know that the answer is love. Believe it, and the game is won." The voice went on to say, *"During the astral interval, everyone makes agreements to be carried out on the earthly plane. During the making of these agreements, most often forget the emotional experience associated with the fulfillment of these agreements. On the earthly plane, you forget you have even made the agreements in the first place. That is why self remembering is so important. No one is to blame for anything that happens to you. You cannot place the blame on some god or devil or your next-door neighbor. Another thing, nobody dies unless he is ready to die. Nobody. Everybody chooses his own way of dying, and each death is as much a statement as birth. You must learn to take responsibility for your thoughts and emotions as well as for your actions, for thoughts fueled by emotions create reality. Your belief system sets the stage, so to speak, and what you see will fall within the parameters of that belief system. Thoughts and emotions, however, are the driving forces."*

"How come nobody knows this stuff?" asked Freemore. "But somebody must know it. And if they do, then why haven't they said something about it before now?"

The reply came, *"The message has been spread throughout the ages. It is the old souls who know, and it is their responsibility to pass the word on to others. There is no judgment here, and ofttimes some overzealous individual goes about setting up a religion. The choice is always up to the individual. It is up to them to accept or reject. A lot of people don't like that because it doesn't leave them an out, someone to blame. A lot of people like rules laid down for them so they will have someone to blame. Their reason is imbedded in fear. The old souls are the ones who have to spread the word. All die, Freemore. Some die better than others and take their knowledge with them. Some live better than others, and their remembrances go with them. Old souls do both."*

Freemore had difficulty believing what he was hearing. He said, "You do know, of course, that this will not be very popular with a lot of people."

"We are not running a popularity contest," said the voice. *"These are truths. We are an ensouled species, just as is man. We have chosen the water as the environment for our development, as you have chosen the land. We–meaning man and dolphins now–are the only ensouled species on this planet. We know it, but you don't. Man hardly believes in his own soul, let alone the*

soul of another species."

"Well, well," said Freemore. "And the minute you are born you are baptized. I like that. Simon, I have a funny feeling that the churches aren't going to like this one bit."

"We don't have time to worry about that," said the dolphin. *"The vibrations are being stepped up in the universe, and the new aeon is about to begin. Those who do not increase their awareness will be left behind for further development. There is actually a move taking place to set up whale farms, if you can believe that. These people would set up human farms, if that was the only source of food. There are major karmic consequences involved in murder, and the killing of a cetacean, be it whale or dolphin, is murder. The same consequences are meted out as for killing and eating a man. No murder is justified–none, period! It is a violation."*

"Man, Simon, if you know all this stuff, why can't you stop it?" Freemore asked. "I mean, if we create our reality, then I suppose you do, also. If that is the case, then why are you allowing yourselves to become victims in this genocide. It doesn't make sense."

"I am here to teach them," Simon replied. *"You are correct, Freemore; there are no victims. Once the realization of that is brought home, then changes will occur, both here and in your world."*

"Is swearing a violation?"

"Of course not."

"What about black magic," Freemore wondered. "Is that evil?"

"There is no good and there is no evil. Forces in the universe attract and repel. An earthquake is neither good nor evil. It is simply an earthquake. Yet, it can kill thousands. Black magic, in itself, is not evil. The karma involved stems from malice or intent. All debts are paid, Freemore. There is a balance in the forces of the universe. If certain forces are invoked, the responsibility lies with the one who invokes them. You must learn responsibility for your thoughts and emotions. These are electromagnetic realities of which you are yet hardly aware. May your thoughts move in peace. I'll get back to you (click, click)."

Freemore had never felt kisses so warm, loving, and giving. "Wake up honey." Phagan was shaking him. "Freemore, wake up. It is almost noon." She leaned over and took his face in her hands.

Opening his eyes, he could not help noticing that her breasts were sweetly, yet discreetly, exposed for his benefit. "You are absolutely beautiful," he murmured.

"Thank you. Brunch is ready, if you're hungry," she said. "I thought we'd have a little champagne, too. Did you sleep well?"

"Like a baby, I think. I have the strangest feeling, though, that I dreamed about Simon. He was telling me something, but now I can't seem to get hold of it. It had to do with teaching and . . . and responsibility, or something like that. Boy, I hate it when I can't remember something, as though it is just out of my grasp and if I could stretch just a little bit more I would have it."

"Well, get up and try stretching while you take your shower. I'll wash your back."

"I have got to try to get a boat, Phagan," Freemore said as he got out of the bed and went to the shower. Squeezing his frame into the tiny area, he said, "The next motor home I buy will have one hell of a big shower in it, I guarantee."

Ignoring his comment, Phagan asked, "What about the boat? Why do you need one?"

"I'd just like to get a little farther out from the beach. I think I would feel more comfortable," he said, turning on the water.

"But didn't you say the dolphins swam up to the old man on the beach?" Phagan asked, then added, "Hand me the soap and I'll do your back."

"They did," Freemore said. "But I have this strange feeling that I need a boat, so I'm going to get one."

"Okay with me. After yesterday, anything you do is okay with me, as long as you're doing it with me."

"Thank you. You don't know how comforting that is to me. Or maybe you do," Freemore added.

"You're welcome," Phagan said. "Let's have brunch. Here, catch!" She threw the bar of soap over his shoulder.

FIVE

"Well, I'll tell you what. I'll trade you my boat for your Winnie over there for one month. I'm not in a hurry to go anywhere, but I would like to take a trip upstate for a bit."

"It's a deal," Freemore said, shaking the kindly old gentleman's hand. "Just let me unload the gear we'll need from the Winnie, and we'll be all set.

"Are you sure you know how to sail?" the old man asked.

"I don't. Well, maybe just a little." Gesturing toward Phagan, Freemore added, "But this gorgeous thing knows everything there is to know about boats."

"Is that true?" asked the elderly gentleman.

"Been sailing all my life. I sailed the Pacific Islands with my parents when I was eighteen."

"That must have been in the last year or two, right?" the old man said with a twinkle in his eye.

"You're sweet," Phagan responded, smiling back at him. "Actually, it was a little longer than that, but maybe only a year or two." She laughed.

"You're a lucky lad, son. Take the boat. And don't worry about the Winnie," said the old man. "I'll take good care of her."

"Likewise," Freemore replied. "By the way, what's her name? I don't see one on her stern."

"Well, to be perfectly honest with you, I haven't named her yet. I've been sort of waiting for the right name to come along, and it just hasn't hit me yet. It will one of these days. When it does, I'll paint the stern. If you get any ideas while you're out there, write them down.

Maybe I'll use one of them."

"Gladly," said Freemore. "We'll see you in a month then."

She was a beautiful ketch, thirty-six feet long with a gold and blue hull and mahogany deck. Below, the spacious cabin afforded ample space for sleeping and dining. Inside was a large mahogany desk for writing. The accompanying cherry wood swivel rocker covered with burgundy velour could be locked in position at the front of the desk. And the kitchen was a gourmet chef's delight, with all the herbs and spices one could think of, along with an assortment of wines secured in their rubber padded rack.

"Can you believe this kitchen?" Freemore said, as much to himself as to Phagan. "Most homes aren't laid out this well."

"First of all, this is not a kitchen," Phagan informed him. "It's a galley. And second of all, I can't believe this whole experience. Can you? I mean, yesterday we were up on that cliff, then after visiting the dolphin, you decided you needed a boat. No problem! We just head south a few miles and you start a conversation with a perfect stranger, who just happens to own a boat, who wants to travel up north for a month, and who doesn't have any transportation, so we trade the Winnebego for his boat and are off into the wild blue yonder in search of your mystical dolphin. The whole thing really freaks me out."

"I've got news; it really freaks me out, too," Freemore said. "But sometimes I get the feeling that we planned this all out a long time ago, so long ago we have both forgotten, and these little events are serving as reminders. Have you noticed experiences of d_j_ vu increasing for you? They are for me. It's as though I'm a little kid again and can see what's going to happen while I'm merrily going along with my life. You know, it just hit me—I think I actually shut a lot of this off because things were too easy, and all the talk I was hearing was telling me that life is supposed to be difficult. Well, you know, it is difficult when you shut yourself off from knowing. Holy cow, Phagan," Freemore exclaimed, turning to face her, "did you hear what I just said? Damn! That's why I shut out the dolphins. That's it! I was listening to everybody else telling me how difficult life was for them, so I thought it was supposed to be that way. Wanting to belong, I shut out the experiences that would allow me to know what was going to happen. How can life be difficult if one knows what is going to happen and can prepare for it? Son of a gun, I've got it! I'm still a little confused about all this having been decided a long time ago, though. I met you only two months ago, you know, yet, I have this feeling that we have been together before. Strange, huh? Actually, I think that dolphin is still the key," Freemore continued. "I'm picking up impressions about the nature of time that I can't seem to put into words, something to do with colors, music, and love. Phagan stay with me on this!" he almost shouted. "This stuff is coming in fast, and I'm trying to interpret . . . It's really coming in fast—colors, music, love, colors, music, love, then tones, tones, tones, feelings, tones, feelings, tones. Phagan, I don't know where this stuff is coming from, but my whole body is beginning to hum. I can feel the humming, and it feels great. Can you hear it? I feel love for everything. I can feel it."

"Something is happening, Freemore," Phagan told him. "You look different." Weeping, she came closer and hugged him. "I love you, Freemore," she said. "I love you."

Then Freemore began to cry, deep, primordial tears, tears a man is never supposed to shed for if he does, he has been told, he is no longer a man. They splashed on the rich mahogany deck of the galley, their saltiness cleansing him. "I love you," he said as they stood in the galley, not knowing what time it was or even if there was such a thing as time. "I can still feel the trembling a little bit," he added. "Was that what you were feeling when we were on the beach?"

"I'm feeling it right now," Phagan answered. "As soon as I came close to you I could feel it. Do you feel any changes in your facial features?"

"No. Why?" Freemore asked, feeling his face with his left hand.

"You look younger. Your face is sort of radiant, glowing almost."

"It feels great, like a cerebral orgasm," he said. "Completely unlike physical sex."

"It's beautiful," Phagan told him. "You know, I've got a feeling the dolphin had something to do with this, and I like it."

The vibrations slowing down, they still clung

to one another. Quietly they went to their bunk. It was not long before they realized that when one was going through the experience, the other could be consumed by it by hugging, and thus picking up on the tones. It carried them into realms hitherto unknown to them. They slept as they had never slept before and in places they had never been. And yet, they were not asleep but awake on the another plane all night.

SIX

The iridescent air filled the blue and gold spinnaker as they headed west, racing the morning sun toward its zenith, the gentle swells of the ocean aiding their voyage. The water sprayed silvery blue-green off the bow, blasting a fine mist of sparkling violet droplets into space.

"The little child within you is sitting within the five-pointed star and rejoices in its knowing." The dolphin swam in circles on top of the water. *"The fire within is the fire that knew how to grow you from a fetus to an adult without your conscious involvement. Thank the source of all that is for that little phenomena,"* it said. *"You, as you understand yourselves, are very limited, and that is the major reason for your fear. Fear is simply a lack of knowledge. If you really knew–I repeat–if you really knew what you were doing, you wouldn't do it. You apply the laws you have been taught, yet steadfastly refute, or try to refute, anything new that comes into your range. Has it ever occurred to you that all true geniuses have considered all the known laws invalid? They didn't like what they saw, so, being inspired, they asked the species to reach for more. You must stretch if you are going to grow. Status quo produces nothing but a stagnant pool. You must be willing to accept what comes to you, acknowledging that you have drawn it to yourself. We are all responsible for our own destinies, as individuals or as a group. What you see you have attracted to yourself, peace or war, love or hate. Know this–hate of war will not stop war; only love of peace will bring peace."*

A silver-red fireball appeared off the port bow approximately fifty yards in front of the boat and maintained that distance between them. The sky had become menacingly black with gigantic, dark, cumulus clouds. The air vibrated with each word spoken, and the clouds undulated at the pauses between the words, as if to show that pauses between the sounds were as important as the sounds themselves. Each thought spoken sent a liquid golden arrow crashing through the surface of the sea directly to the overhanging clouds, blazing a trail of light through the black void. For a long moment, the blazing trail hung there, then suddenly an explosive brilliance shattered the sky and the threatening clouds disappeared.

"This is getting really spooky, Phagan," Freemore said, "really spooky. First, the clouds, then those spears coming out of the water and shooting toward the clouds. What's going on?"

"I think Simon is demonstrating that we are creating our reality."

"Now what the hell is that supposed to mean out here in the middle of the damned ocean?"

"Somehow we both let our thoughts and emotions get a little dark, or rather, black. Did you see the size of that cloud? You must have been getting quite ticked off about something to cause such a huge monster."

"Me?" declared Freemore. "Couldn't it possibly have been you? Why does it have to be me?"

From somewhere in the water came the reply, *"Actually, it was both of you. The collective thoughts and emotions of everyone form struc-*

tures upon the astral plane. As intensities peak, the result precipitates toward your reality. The event experienced is both individual and collective, for what is perceived is never the same for any two people."

"Simon!" Phagan shouted. "Is that you Simon?"

"You'd better hope it is," Freemore whispered.

"We are here with you, and now that you have had your first lesson, we will continue," said the voice. *"Your thoughts and emotions, in conjunction with your beliefs, create your reality, all of it, every little bit of it, even to the weather. Now, what you perceive as cause and effect is simply a myopic view of the whole. There is only cause and effect if you believe there to be, for the nature of time and of the universe is that all time is one. Everything is happening at once, yet, you are situated so you perceive a linear relationship. The result is that you say so and so causes such and such."*

"If that is the case, then how can you say we created the weather?" Freemore asked.

"This may seem strange to you," said the dolphin, *"but . . ."*

"No kidding!" exclaimed Freemore. "The whole thing seems strange to me."

The dolphin went on. *"I have been guilty of that type of humor myself. I shall continue. You – and I am referring now to your race as a whole–have all made agreements to appear in space and time such as it seemed to you at the moment. These agreements are what caused your inner self to seek certain experiences so it could enjoy the physical experience of the flesh. At each moment in your time, you have the choice to realize the truth, and until you do, you will seem to be at the mercy of circumstances.*

"You have a question, Freemore. Go ahead."

"Do all dolphins understand this stuff?"

"Some do, some don't. All do know, however, that they are an ensouled species, just as are humans. The rub comes when human population en masse does not even believe in a soul, much less believe there might be an ensouled species on the planet with them. Now don't take this wrong, Freemore and Phagan, but the nature of your time is that man has yet to learn the sacredness of all life."

"What about karma?"

"Karma is associated with the nature of time. Until you understand that you create your reality by yourself, in conjunction with the thoughts and emotions of others, you will feel you are at the mercy of events, and that includes karma. All time is one, and when you learn to move and act in real space, you will understand that truth is the highest good and that love is the highest truth."

"My brain is burning up with all this," Freemore said. He gazed out across the water. "Phagan," he said, "are you making any sense out of this?"

"I'm just listening," she replied. "I think I

could listen to him all night."

"Listening is fine," responded the dolphin, *"for one must learn. There is a time for doing, however, and that is the reason you are both out here."*

"Oh, great! I should have known there was going to be a catch to all this," said Freemore. Then remembering, he added, "By the way, what ever happened to that old man you were talking to on the beach when I was a little boy?"

"We'll get to that soon enough, Freemore, soon enough. As far as the catch is concerned, it is simply a matter of my remembering our agreement and your having forgotten. Part of the agreement was for me to remind you of the reason for your journey in this space and time and to provide the impetus for you to fulfill the other agreements you have made. The choice is still yours, however."

"How could I have made an agreement with a dolphin? And when did we make this so-called agreement?"

Phagan spoke up. "Freemore," she said, "if you don't stop talking so sharply to Simon you will really tick me off. I'm surprised he hasn't just chucked the whole thing and left you for another lifetime."

"You're right. I'm sorry, Simon," Freemore said. "I guess it's . . . well, it's so damned confusing."

"The agreement was with the essence, Freemore," the dolphin explained. *"The essence doesn't care how long it takes for it knows the*

nature of time. Actually, the agreement has not been made in your terms of time. Does that make things a little more simple?" The dolphin paused, then continued. *"My turn for a little humor. By the way, I knew in the future that you were a stubborn fellow–witty, but stubborn. I always did like challenges, though, and so does Phagan. I'll get back to you (click, click)."*

SEVEN

Phagan had brought the ketch about and they headed back toward the coast. Each lost in his own thoughts on their journey back to the real world, neither had said a word since Simon's *"click, click."* Phagan was first to break the silence.

"Did you get all that?" she asked. "I mean, did you really get all that?"

"Get all what? All I can remember right now is the click, click. My mind is ablaze, and that's all I'm sure of at the moment. There was so much shouting at me and through me that I can't remember what was said or who said it."

"How do you feel? Do you feel anything strange happening to your body?" she asked as she gave Freemore a gentle hug.

"Do you have to ask?"

"If you don't answer the question, you'll be in for a cold night," she teased, pressing her head against his shoulder.

"Somehow, I have a feeling this is bordering on blackmail."

"No bordering about it." She looked up into his face and smiled.

"That's what I thought. Actually, I'm not sure exactly what I felt," Freemore told her, resting his chin on the top of her head. "Sort of scared, I guess. This 'You create your own reality' stuff can scare the crap out of a person, if it's the truth. Gees, think of it–there wouldn't be anyone to blame for anything. No wonder the churches don't talk about this stuff."

"Listen to me carefully, dummy. Read my lips. What physical sensations did you feel when that dolphin was talking?"

"Oh, okay," Freemore said. "My stomach is

sort of cramped up tight, like the skin of a drum. I don't feel any pain, but it's as though there's something inside me that wants to talk to that dolphin personally. Weird, huh? I feel as though I'm on an incredible high, too–nice feelings. I didn't really want him to leave. I'm sorry for avoiding your question, but this stuff is getting pretty heavy for me. I hope you've got it all figured out."

"Me? For crying out loud, this is your quest, lover," Phagan exclaimed. "I didn't even know about this stuff until I met you."

"I know, or at least, I thought I did. That dolphin, though, obviously thinks the two of us were meant to work something out, and I'll be damned if I can figure it out. So that leaves you, my precious, precocious beauty."

"Well," said Phagan, "there have been some strange things happening that I haven't told you about. I've been seeing flashes of lights, like crystal globes tinged with red gold. Sometimes the whole sky seems to be filled with them."

"You might be seeing what some of the experts have an unusual name for. I can't remember now what they call them, but they're supposed to be the life-giving forces themselves in their purest form. I can remember seeing them as a kid around the trees and plants. I even thought I saw little people using them to help plants and animals grow. It was neat to watch."

"Freemore, could it be that those globes are used by the 'child within,' of which Simon speaks, to keep us growing and functioning?"

"Might be. I never thought of that," Freemore replied. "You know," he continued, "if that is the case, then we are actually forming our physical bodies with our thoughts and emotions—I mean, with the ones we accept as ours. That little guy is doing what we want done and going after those particles that will best do the job. How does that sound?"

The voice coming from the water again almost startled the two. *"Some of your scientists are close, but they must begin to look at the pauses between the events,"* said the dolphin. *"The electrons blink on and off, but you just don't know it yet. Events blink on and off, and neither do you know that yet. Also, you yourselves blink on and off, but you don't know that yet, either."*

"It's a good thing you are born baptized, Simon, or you would really be in trouble," Freemore laughed.

"I'll get back to you (click, click)." The dolphin swam away.

Phagan watched as the violet silver glow disappeared into the blue-green depths of the sea. "Thank you for the insight, Simon," she shouted. Then turning to Freemore, she asked, "Where did he come from? I didn't even begin to feel his presence until I heard him."

"Blinked on?"

"Why that cheeky little devil," laughed Phagan.

Freemore said, "You know, this is actually beginning to be fun. This is great! We are actually experiencing spiritual truths that are, as I get it, simple, not complex as others would have us believe."

"Freemore, how far is it to the coast?" asked Phagan. "Do you have any idea?"

"We're about seventy miles out right now, I figure," he replied. "We'll probably have to spend the night at sea. We'll never make it in before sunset."

"I think I'll turn in now. Okay? I'm really getting a little sleepy."

"Go ahead," Freemore told her. "Everything is fine here."

"Even without me?" she teased.

"Well, not that fine, but I'll manage."

Starting for the bunk, Phagan said, "If that dolphin shows up, give me a holler."

"No sweat," he agreed. "Now get down below before you fall overboard. You're so out you're staggering."

"Remember, wake me up if that dolphin comes by again," she reminded him once more.

"I'll remember, I'll remember."

Standing alone on the deck, Freemore looked out over the water and said softly, "She's beautiful. One can tell she's a Leo for she has that golden aura about her. Thinking back to when we were boarding at the dock, she had ships and men going in all directions. One old salt even took out two slips because he wasn't watching where he was going. She waved to him as he grounded himself on the third slip." Freemore chuckled and said a little louder, "What do you think, Simon? Simon, are you there?" There was no answer.

"Boy, when the sun goes down, it gets dark, and I mean real dark! This compass had better not start acting up or I am going to be in deep trouble," Freemore muttered to himself. "Man, I can't even see the water." The only sound he had to keep him company was the slapping of the waves on the hull of the ketch.

"Be careful, Freemore, for you create your own reality," came the voice.

"Simon?" Freemore asked in a loud whisper. "Phagan, wake . . ."

"Quiet, Freemore," said the dolphin. *"She's asleep. She'll be getting the information in a dream state. With any luck, she may even join us later."*

"What do you mean "with any luck?" That sounds a little iffy to me. Is she going to be all right?"

"There is nothing to worry about, Freemore. It just depends on her willingness to join us. Now, if I may say so, we, as dolphins, have advanced to a point where we know how to handle images. We know how to handle thoughts, and some of us have learned how to handle emotions. It is time to reacquaint you with the knowledge you had when you were forming your physical body in your mother's womb. It was your choice then, and it is your choice now. Thoughts fueled by emotions create your reality. They mix and merge with the thoughts of others, like attracting like. Your emotions trigger certain chemical

reactions within your being. These chemical reactions generate electrical impulses that send messages to the force you call God. There is always an answer to every request, but it might not always be the answer you desire. The fault lies not with the gift but with the method of the request. Man has trouble communicating among his own species for the same reason. Your agreement, Freemore, was to get at least a portion of this message across to the minds of men. The dolphins don't understand why they are having so much trouble with this, and that is one of the reasons I am here. You, my friend, are the other. The dolphin knows from whence he came, and he understands the theory of relativity. Man and dolphins are the otters of the universe. Dolphins know it, but men don't . . . yet. Are you with me, Freemore?"

"Not quite, but I'll get it," Freemore replied.

Suddenly Phagan appeared beside him, having come up through the floor of the deck. "Simon, what . . . ," Freemore had begun to say, but at her appearance, he exclaimed, "Phagan, are you okay?"

"I'm fine." She moved over and put an arm around him. "Are you all right?" she asked. "You look as though you've seen a ghost."

"Very funny," he said. "Very, very funny. What are you doing? Do you remember how you got here?"

"Of course I do. I came up through the deck."

"What are you doing, coming up through the

deck? Is this some kind of dream?"

"It's called astral projection, silly. And Simon is helping me out, so to speak. I'm supposed to teach you the next time we're in bed together."

"I can't wait for that one," Freemore said.

With that, she disappeared back through the deck.

Freemore said, "Sim . . ."

"Hold the questions, Freemore," the dolphin said. *"I've got more to say, and you'll have plenty of time to ask Phagan all the questions you want. She has the answers now. As you get the word out, stress always the here and now, for that is the point of power. For your information, truths are not in the sequence of events that can be predicted but in those events that do not seem to have plausible answers. When you are looking for truth, look where nobody else is looking. If you look where they are looking, you will become lost in their egos. It has been said many, many times before in many, many ways–look within thyself. Knowing that you create your world will allow you to choose your destiny with freedom. Contact that original force that knew you before you were a seed within your father. That beautiful spark is still there, now, waiting. May your thoughts move in peace. I'll get back to you (click, click)."*

A white phosphor glow surrounded the boat. Through it, Freemore counted thirteen dolphins leaping and twirling, diving and dancing between two worlds. Lights and letters flashed through the black night, leaving violet trails of the dolphins thoughts. He watched as the thoughts mixed and merged within the violet haze, each looking for its counterpart, and finally, combining and cascading into the world from whence it had come. A silver-gold dolphin rose high out of the sea, sending a beam of light from its eyes to Freemore's. Thoughts flowed through that beam of light, and Freemore felt a tidal wave of love flow through him.

"All worlds are created the same way, Freemore," the dolphin told him. *"We prefer peace, and since we know how it works, we work at it."*

"Now, who are you?" Freemore asked. "Are you a friend of Simon?"

"Simon and I are more than friends, Freemore. We are, as you call it, soul mates. Everybody has one."

"Soul mates? What's going on?"

"You'll find out," said the dolphin.

"When?"

"Actually, you've already found out, but you don't know it yet. You've found out in your future. As Simon told you, all time is one. That's why you should concentrate on the here and now. We know it, and if you truly understood the theory of relativity, you would know it, too."

"Do you have a name," asked Freemore, "or do I call you Simonette?"

"Listen to the tone of our being and you'll know my name," said the voice from the water. *"You'll also find out your true name. Listen to*

your tone, Freemore, for it is in tune with the tone of the universe. Let every atom and molecule, every consciousness in your body, sing with the universal tone. We are all one, Freemore. Love is the highest truth, and the nature of truth is that it always wins. May your thoughts move in peace (click, click)."

EIGHT

Freemore hurried below deck to get Phagan and tell her what had just happened, but he found her still asleep. He decided he should let her sleep, not knowing what that astral projection stuff was all about. Besides, for all he knew, she could still be out practicing with Simon. Climbing the ladder, he went back up to the deck to think about what had happened and what he had heard.

Suddenly he was overcome by a feeling of something akin to a cone of whirling white fuzz spinning above and inside his head at the same time. Settling back against the port bulkhead, he closed his eyes and said, "Maybe this is what it feels like to be going crazy. The only question I have is–how will I know when I get there?" Opening his eyes, he saw the blackness of the night was pierced by the light of the milky way, billions of suns sending their flickering light to the little planet earth, giving comfort and succor through the night, as if to say, "You are not alone, little one."

"Well, Simonette, you really scrambled my brains with that soul mate stuff and 'listen to your tone.' Okay, I'll listen."

Freemore sat at the wheel all night listening, catching catnaps, and then snapping awake to listen again. He listened and listened and listened and heard nothing except the wind and the waves. Finally, just as the sun was cracking the horizon, burning the darkness with its light, it happened. After sailing all night, they were about two hundred yards from shore. He could hear the waves breaking and rolling toward the beach.

"We perceive your thoughts as lights," came the familiar voice. *"They form patterns. Look toward the shore."*

Just then Phagan came up on the deck.

Freemore put his finger to his lips, indicating for her to be quiet, and pointed toward the shore. There, ranging from about fifty to a thousand feet above the ground, were patterns of light rising upward as single units and joining together in larger and larger clusters. The more brilliant colors rose higher and were fewer. The heavy blacks and browns barely got off the ground and almost kept the more beautiful colors from lifting off. When the lights could not rise any higher, they fell swiftly to earth, a tidal wave of thoughts and emotions spreading across the land, creating reality for people even as they slept.

"It's absolutely incredible!" Freemore said. "Phagan, did you see what I saw?"

"Beautiful and frightening at the same time, isn't it?" Phagan replied in awe. "I can still see them, can't you?"

"No, I think I've lost the tone," Freemore said. "I'll just have to learn to keep the pitch, so to speak." Turning, he put his arms around Phagan and said, "You sure had a nice nap. When are you going to tell me all about that astral projection stuff?" He smiled down at her.

"As I said, I'm going to teach you. We'll start our first lesson tonight. How will that be?"

"Fine by me."

"Always remember, thoughts are things," said the voice in the distance. *"When you are traveling astrally, keep in mind that the colors you see are the emotions on that level. Thoughts of love bring love; thoughts of peace bring peace. By the way,"* the voice continued, *"did you hear*

the name of the golden one, Freemore?"

"Her name is Isis." The instant the thought of saying the name came to Freemore, thousands of dolphins broke the surface of the water, gyrating, twisting, and turning amid millions of shrilling clicks. Ecstasy filled the air as dolphin after dolphin leaped over the boat from port to starboard and from starboard to port. There were as many in the air as there were in the water. They stayed until each had looked directly into the eyes of the two humans in the boat, thoughts of love and peace passing from inner self to inner self.

Phagan's eyes filled with tears as she said, "I love these beautiful creatures, Freemore. I love them." Then hugging Freemore, she shouted at the top of her lungs, "I love you all! Thank you, Simon and Isis, for giving me myself."

"We are social creatures of reason, Freemore, and we have an extremely rich emotional life. Phagan has experienced this in her workings at the astral level," said the voice from the sea. *"We have a strong sense of personal loyalty. We understand responsibility, individually, en masse, and to the source of all. In other words, Freemore, we cooperate; we do not compete. We go out of our way to help other species. Incidentally,"* the voice added, *"we do not take pets. Now it is time for you to pass the word. One more thing–look to the north, Freemore. See that silver speck out there just above the horizon?*

"I see it, yes."

"Concentrate on it," the voice instructed.

"Ask to know your purpose for being here. Forgive everyone for everything, totally and completely, without qualifications of any kind. Ask forgiveness for yourself, and then ask 'Why am I here?' Remember to let the inner self speak. May your thoughts move in peace."

Doing exactly as Simon had said, Freemore concentrated on the silver speck and forgave everyone for everything, without qualifications of any kind, and he asked for forgiveness for himself. Then he shouted, "Why am I here?"

To this day, Phagan and Freemore cannot get over the incredible phenomena that occurred. As they watched the silver speck, it started to move toward them, growing into a beam of brilliant white light. As it came closer, they could see it was building itself out of other brilliant particles in its path, each particle rapidly being attracted into the beam and itself becoming a part of the beam. The speed was unbelievable.

When it struck Freemore between his eyes, Phagan screamed and covered his face, but he kept looking up the beam. Its other end opened, and he saw standing at the other end of the light the old man who had been on the beach, the little boy, and his present self. It was then he realized he and the old man were one and the same person, the old man returning to show the boy, and the boy there to bring them together once again. The boy still lived. The old man still lived. Phagan and Freemore were married, so obviously, Freemore still lived.

The purpose of Freemore's story? You are

reading about it. And as for Phagan teaching him astral projection, well, he promises to see you in your dreams.

Freemore could think of only one name for the boat–May your thoughts move in peace; I'll get back to you.

OTHER BOOKS
by
ARTHUR FANNING

Souls, Evolution and the Father
by Lord God Jehovah
channeled through
Arthur Fanning

Information about the creation of souls, the purpose of evolution and the history of mankind on planet Earth.

Light Technology Publishing
P.O. Box 1526
Sedona, AZ 86336
ISBN 0-929385-32-2 $14.95